Conservative Personal Finance:

A Guide to Total Debt Elimination

Gregory L Bonnette

Library of Congress Cataloging-in-Publication Data

Bonnette, Gregory L.

Conservative Personal Finance: A Guide to Total Debt Elimination

ISBN-13: 978-1505809046

Visit us at www.conservativepersonalfinance.com

Manufactured in the United States of America

Disclaimer
The information in this guide is distributed on an "as is" basis. Although every effort has been made to provide accurate information, the author of this manual is not responsible for financial loss, or purported financial loss, which may occur in the process of attempting to implement any of the strategies or ideas contained in this publication. Every individual is responsible for the results of his own financial decisions. As financial advice should be tailored to the specific circumstances of each individual, nothing provided herein should be used as a substitute for the advice of a competent financial advisor.

* * * *

To my wife and kids, the reason for this book

Table of Contents

Introduction

The straightforward steps laid out in the next few chapters will help save you both time and money. They'll also give you a new measure of control and feeling of comfort over your finances. The trick is to reduce your expenses and debts so that you have the maximum possible disposable income to save and invest. You want to be using your time and money to become wealthy and independent, instead of making that happen for someone else. Consider every area of your life where you could reduce your expenses. The chapter titled "Controlling Your Spending" deals with strategies to do this. This guide covers topics such as concentration, relaxation, direct deposit, good versus bad debt, and spending plan techniques (psychologically better than a budget), automatic bill payment and debit, and using spreadsheets to keep track of your debts and spending plan progress. Finally, you will see links to websites and names of computer programs that are helpful in keeping track of and reducing your debt, saving money and how to give back once you're on good financial footing.

In today's world, with the prices of goods and services skyrocketing, we all need as much knowledge as we can get to stay out of debt. This knowledge is not easy to come by. This guide draws together knowledge and techniques based on actual experience.

Many people believe they need to spend a great deal of money to obtain such information. But, if you are already in debt why should you pay hundreds of dollars for advice on how to get out of it? This system will easily save you hundreds, or even thousands, of dollars depending on your situation and willingness to follow even a small fraction of its advice. No matter how much debt you have, following these strategies will help you to reduce or eliminate your debt quicker than you ever thought possible.

This is not a program to get debts cancelled or for some agency to ask your creditors to lower your interest rates for you, that doesn't work. You have to do the work. You have to take the time to go through these steps and get these things done yourself. Part of the beauty of this guide is that it teaches you lessons about personal finance, debt and credit that you can use the rest of your life. Let's get started.

Chapter 1

Concentrate!!!

Concentration is key when trying to get a handle on, and control of, your finances. If you can't concentrate, you can't keep track of them. Learning to concentrate will have a profound effect on every aspect of your life, not just your finances.

Chapter 2

Relax!!!

Relaxation is important in order to have the energy to get a handle on your finances. If you can't relax, then you're wasting precious energy needed to concentrate on your finances. I find that those with the worst money troubles are usually the most uptight and nervous people you could ever meet, myself included.

We all know the sick feeling we get in our stomach before an important presentation or performance. We all get the sweaty palms, increased heart rate, and the sense of angst that we feel as these events approach. We've all felt our hearts pounding, and the tension and angst that come when we face frustration over trying to work out our life's goals.

This section briefly gives you some good techniques for managing the fight-or-flight response that lies behind these feelings. "Imagery" is the first of these. As well as being a powerful mental rehearsal technique, it is also useful for relaxing when you are under pressure. Meditation, self-hypnosis and use of relaxation CD's are also good ways of relaxing. Finally, deep breathing, progressive muscular relaxation, and the relaxation response are useful physical techniques for managing muscular tension.

Imagery - Mental Stress Management

Imagery is a potent method of stress reduction, especially when combined with physical relaxation methods such as deep breathing.

You're aware of how particular environments can be very relaxing, while others can be extremely stressful. The idea behind the use of imagery in stress reduction is that you use your imagination to enjoy and recreate a situation that is very relaxing. The more deeply you imagine the situation, the more relaxing the experience will be.

With imagery, you replace actual experience with scenes from your imagination. Your body physically reacts to these imagined scenes as if they were real.

To relax with imagery, imagine a safe, warm, comfortable and pleasant place that you can enjoy in your imagination.

Using biofeedback equipment that measures body stress has shown that imagery works. By imagining pleasant and unpleasant scenes, you can actually see or hear the changing levels of stress in your body.

Meditation – Relaxing with sustained concentration

As with the next tool (self-hypnosis), meditation has a popular image that can lead to it being dismissed as a less-than-serious stress management tool. This is a shame. Good research has been conducted into meditation that shows it is a useful and practical technique for managing stress.

As with the next two tools, meditation is a good way of relaxing during, and at the end of, a stressful day. It's something you can learn to do yourself, or may be something you prefer to learn in classes.

Meditation is a useful and practical relaxation technique. To use it, sit in a comfortable place, close your eyes, relax your body, and focus your concentration on something for a period of time.

By meditating, you rest your body, allow stress hormones to subside and occupy your mind so that unpleasant, stressful thoughts don't interrupt.

Self-Hypnosis

Like meditation, hypnosis has a dubious image. Many people over the years have made their living by overlaying this practical and useful technique with unwarranted mystical and magical rituals. In fact, it is a useful tool for achieving deep relaxation.

Typical self-hypnosis sessions can last between 15 and 25 minutes; however, they can last for as long as you like.

Physical Techniques: Deep breathing, progressive muscular relaxation & The Relaxation Response

This tool introduces three useful physical relaxation techniques that can help you reduce muscle tension and manage the effects of the fight-or-flight response on your body. This is particularly important if you need to think clearly and perform precisely when you are under pressure.

The techniques we'll look at are Deep Breathing, Progressive Muscular Relaxation and The Relaxation Response.

Deep Breathing, Progressive Muscular Relaxation, and the steps leading to the Relaxation Response are three good techniques that can help you to relax your body and manage the symptoms of the fight-or-flight response.

These are particularly helpful for handling nerves prior to an important performance, and for calming down when you are highly stressed.

Relaxation & the Relaxation Response

The relaxation response may help people to counteract the toxic effects of chronic stress by slowing breathing rate, relaxing muscles, and reducing blood pressure.

Multitasking has become a part of our everyday lives. At any given time, most of us are actively working on, or overseeing, a handful of projects and problems all at once, making it nearly impossible to slow down and relax.

All of the above relaxation techniques are readily available for reading on the web. No matter what you do to relax, It's very important that you find some way to do it to be able to concentrate on your spending, your debts, and getting on your way to paying them off.

Chapter 3

Debt – Good vs. Bad

Unfortunately for most of us, debt is a way of life. Most of us have it, though some have been fortunate enough to have little or none. It's almost impossible to live debt-free. Most of us can't pay cash for our homes or our children's college education's. Too many of us let debt get out of hand. However, when it comes to debt, there is a big difference between good and bad debt.

An example of good debt would be a mortgage. A home can be sold for more than its cost, given the right conditions. Student loans are considered good debt because they provide debtors with the opportunity to educate themselves in order to make a better living. In addition, the interest on these kinds of debt is usually tax deductible. Mortgages and student loans are considered good debt because they tend to increase your value or net worth.

Credit card debt is generally the worst kind, since it carries the highest interest rates. If not used carefully, credit card debt can add up fast, especially when you carry a balance beyond your grace period, when the interest starts accruing. It's far too easy to spend more than you can afford, especially when you pay by credit card. The average U.S. household with at least one credit card carries nearly a $9,000 balance and personal bankruptcies have hit record highs in recent years. Other examples of bad debt are car loans and personal loans. These types of loans not only carry high interest rates, but usually the value of whatever you have purchased begins to depreciate immediately.

According to most banks your total monthly long-term debt payments, including your mortgage and credit cards, should not exceed 36 percent of your gross monthly income. More likely, though, if your total monthly payments to creditors, utilities, food, clothes, and so forth, is anywhere near your total take-home pay, you're getting in over your head. It is better to figure out your necessary monthly expenses, like food, entertainment, clothes, diapers for the kids and so on (a spending plan). Once this number is established, the rest goes toward debt payoff. Ignore the rules for "acceptable" levels of debt. Don't be a slave to your money. If you allow yourself to get so far in debt that you have nothing left over after all your monthly debt obligations are met, you may never get out of debt again. Start now. Set a limit that is comfortable for you, one that allows you to pay all your bills AND pay an extra amount on your debt that will help you to eventually get out of debt completely.

Of course, avoiding debt at all cost may not be smart either, if it means depleting your reserves needed for emergencies. The challenge is learning how to judge which debt makes sense and which does not, and then wisely managing the money you must borrow.

Chapter 4

Controlling Your Spending

The first thing to do to control debt is to get a handle on your spending. Figure out where and on what your income is being spent. To do this, separate your expenses into two categories. The first is everyday expenses (discretionary), the second is required debt payments (non-discretionary). Some suggestions for reducing discretionary expenses are to:

- **STOP ALL CREDIT CARD SPENDING** (you should only be using them for emergencies)
- Keep a notebook with you to record even the smallest expense, like coffee in the morning
- Look for alternative products when shopping at the grocery store
- Look for alternative grocery stores, discount stores and bulk food clubs
- Lower the temperature on your hot water heater to 120 degrees F.
- Lower your thermostat
- Turn off lights when not in use, use energy efficient lights
- Look for alternative energy suppliers
- Look for the lowest gas prices within a reasonable driving distance
- Keep your car tuned up to save fuel
- Clip coupons
- Avoid the Laundromat. If possible, buy a washer and dryer (energy efficient ones)
- Start a garden with your most commonly eaten vegetables in it
- Eat at home whenever possible
- Don't waste leftovers (use re-sealable containers)
- Bring your lunch to work
- Make sure you're giving as little of your income to the IRS as possible every payday by adjusting your deductions so when tax time comes you owe nothing. Use this extra money to pay down debts
- Buy large items during sales

Some suggestions for reducing non-discretionary expenses are to:

- Call all your creditors and ask them to lower your interest rates

- Transfer your balances to lower interest cards (but be careful to read the fine print)
- Choose a credit card that allows you to earn miles or money. Then simply make charges to your credit card that you already intend to pay off that month, such as car insurance, utilities and cable. All of these normal expenses could be charged to your credit card and paid off that month. You get the miles or money without accumulating debt. Do this only if you are sure you can pay off your cards balance every month.
- Get a debt consolidation loan (then cancel some credit cards) but only if you can first change your spending habits (if it does not extend debt and payments!)
- Look for cheaper car and homeowners insurance rates annually

Avoid declaring bankruptcy. It will likely put you in a worse situation than you are already in. Declaring bankruptcy can ruin your credit for a long time and make it almost impossible for you to get any credit whatsoever if you need it during that time. Declare bankruptcy only if <u>absolutely</u> necessary, and only after talking to a professional credit counselor about your situation. Many times, they can help you in ways you never thought of and maybe even help you avoid going the bankruptcy route.

Chapter 5

Spending Plans

This topic sounds a lot like budgeting, but it isn't. A spending plan may be a better idea than a budget. A spending plan is different from a budget because in a spending plan you try to look forward a month and figure out where your income needs to be spent. With a budget you're always using the same amounts. Using this technique, at the end of the month, you have money left over to spend on paying off debts. Budgets are hard to follow. There is a psychological factor at play here. With a budget, it feels like you are constantly depriving yourself of something because you are always basing the budget on past expenses, which may no longer be the same. In a spending plan, you are looking forward and trying to figure out where in the future you will spend your income, which is a much more positive way of looking at your spending.

Spending plans involve looking forward a month, or more, and figuring out what bills and expenses are coming up. Say, for instance, you have to register your car again or it's time to get your pet checked out at the vet. A budget doesn't usually take these things into consideration, but a spending plan does. Keeping track of future expenses is a very good way to know what you need to set aside in the future. It's very easy to do this if you use the personal spending plan spreadsheet shown below.

Once you have a spending plan worked out, you can then figure out what amount to deposit into your bank account that is dedicated only to paying bills (discussed in the next chapter).

Diagram 1 – Personal Spending Plan Spreadsheet

Personal Spending Plan													
Category	Jan	Feb	Mar	Apr	May	Jun	Jul	Aug	Sep	Oct	Nov	Dec	Total
Income													
Wages													$0.00
Int./div.													$0.00
Misc.													$0.00
Tot. Income	$0.00	$0.00	$0.00	$0.00	$0.00	$0.00	$0.00	$0.00	$0.00	$0.00	$0.00	$0.00	$0.00
Misc. payments													
Car Loan													$0.00
Stud, Loan													$0.00
JS Loan													$0.00
Misc. Totals													$0.00
	Jan	Feb	Mar	Apr	May	Jun	Jul	Aug	Sep	Oct	Nov	Dec	Year
Tot. Expense	$0.00	$0.00	$0.00	$0.00	$0.00	$0.00	$0.00	$0.00	$0.00	$0.00	$0.00	$0.00	$0.00
Cash extra/(short)	$0.00	$0.00	$0.00	$0.00	$0.00	$0.00	$0.00	$0.00	$0.00	$0.00	$0.00	$0.00	$0.00

Chapter 6

Roll Down Method of Controlling Debt

This method is basically taking a set amount of money (the minimum payment for that debt **plus** whatever you can spare), paying off a debt, then taking that same amount plus the amount you are paying to the next debt and paying that debt off and so on until you get all your debts paid off. Using this method in conjunction with the other techniques in this guide, you will be able to quickly reduce your personal debt. There are many variations on this method. They depend on such things as your interest rates, amounts owed to each creditor, and whether they're secured or unsecured debts. The basic premise of this method is that once you get a debt paid off, you take what you were paying to that creditor and put it towards paying off the next one in line and never reducing the total amount you are paying to all your creditors until you are debt free. Determining which order to pay your debts off in is the tricky part. Normally it would be advantageous to pay your highest interest rate debts off first, then the next highest, and so on, until they're all paid off. Although this sounds like the best course of action, sometimes it is not. Instead of giving specific examples that probably won't exactly fit your situation, here are the general steps to follow:

1. Make a list of your debtors, the amount you owe and the corresponding interest rates.

2. Try to figure out how much extra money you can put towards paying off your debts (diagram 2, blue highlighted amounts).

3. Start a spreadsheet with as many tabs as there are debtors to be paid. On each sheet, run an amortization table for the highest interest rate debt. Continue doing this until you have each debt laid out in this fashion, one to each sheet, in order from highest interest rate to lowest.

4. Add the extra amount you can afford to each payment for the highest interest rate debt until you come to a date when it's finally paid off.

5. Add the amount of the payment you were making on the previous debt to the payments for the next debt, starting on the date in which you got the previous debt paid off. Continue this until it's paid off.

6. Repeat step 4 until all debts are paid off.

7. Repeat steps 3 through 6, but this time, instead of listing them in order from highest interest to lowest, list them in order from smallest amount owed to biggest.

8. From these two spreadsheets, choose the method that fits your situation best.

The second method may not be the cheapest way to go, but it will still save you lots of money over what you're probably doing right now. The advantage to the second method is that, although it may or may not cost more or take longer than the first method to pay off your debts, psychologically, it will help you to keep on track. Getting the first debt paid off quickly feels good and makes you more likely to stick with it. You can also choose to use any combination of the two methods. Sometimes situations change and for whatever reason you might have to adjust your strategy accordingly. It's OK to do this if it helps keep you on track toward paying off your debt.

Diagram 2 - Sample Debt Calculator Spreadsheet – Required Deposits

Credit/Debit	Monthly	Bi-Weekly
Total Pay	$2,367.02	$1,092.47
Total Deposit to other Account	$1,083.33	$500.00
Car Ins.	$52.50	$24.23
Car Loan	$132.78	$61.28
Loan 1	$52.83	$24.38
Student Loan	$0.00	$0.00
Mortgage Loan	$687.10	$317.12
Satellite	$38.98	$17.99
Loan 2	$67.12	$30.98
Total Debt	$2,114.64	$975.99
Leftover	$252.38	$116.48
VISA	$252.38	$116.48
Total Deposit to BA Account	$1,283.69	$592.47

Chapter 7

Automatic Bill Payments

One technique to avoid bouncing checks and having to pay late payment fees is to use automatic bill payment to pay creditors. This is not about letting creditors deduct money from your account, but setting up a bank account from which your bank makes scheduled payments. You set the dates, the amounts and the frequency. This way you can keep track of what is being paid, and when, ahead of time. You normally wouldn't use this technique to pay bills that vary in amounts, like utility bills or credit card payments. The reason is that you might forget to set the correct amount and risk not paying enough, which will cost you with very expensive late fees.

Use this as a memory tool. If you have a bad memory, like many of us do, taking steps like these will help you to remember to pay bills on time, saving you loads of money. Use a spreadsheet to keep track of what's being deposited and withdrawn, then set this account up with all the payments that need to be made regularly. You may even wish to keep track for a year in advance, so if something is going to bounce, you can catch it ahead of time and have time to correct the error. The steps are straightforward. I will outline them in the next chapter.

Chapter 8

Using a Spreadsheet to Track Debts

Follow the steps below to keep track of recurring bill payments:

1. Compile a list of all monthly recurring bills and the minimum amount due for each.

2. Take these amounts and add them together.

3. Multiply the result by 12 (the number of months in a year), then divide by the number of pay periods each year (a good example would be if you're paid every other week, you would divide the result by 26).

4. Add the amount from the chapter titled "Roll Down Method of Controlling Debt", step 2 to the result of step 3 above.

5. The result from step 4 above is the **minimum** amount of money you need to deposit into the account each pay period (direct deposit is best for this since it automates the deposits, keeping you from forgetting).

6. Arrange these amounts in a spreadsheet by date. Set the spreadsheet up so that the last column gives you the balance after each deposit or debit (see diagram 3).

7. You will probably get one or more negative results at some point, the key to this is that the **largest negative** result you get is the minimum amount that needs to be in the account to begin with (for example, in diagram 3, the TOTAL column shows in red the **minimum** needed in the account to start).

8. Now, set up direct deposit with your employer, the bank account with the beginning deposit and all of your automatic, repeating deposits and payments.

This method works great if strictly abided by. When payment amounts change, for whatever reason, simply repeat the steps outlined above and make sure nothing will bounce. Another important rule to stick to is to **NEVER** withdraw cash from this account. If you do it once or twice, then replenish it as soon as possible, you *might* be OK. However, this can become habit forming very easily and will eventually lead to bounced payments and late fees again, which are the very things you're trying to avoid in the first place.

Diagram 3 - Sample Debt Calculator Spreadsheet (Step 6)

	Bank America Bank		
	Beginning Balance =======>		$200.00
DATE	ITEM	+/-	TOTAL
1/1/2014	Car Loan	($132.78)	$67.22
1/2/2014	Bank Deposit	$500.00	$567.22
1/4/2014	Car Insurance	($105.00)	$462.22
1/15/2014	Loan 1	($52.83)	$409.39
1/15/2014	Bank Deposit	$500.00	$909.39
1/27/2014	Mortgage Payment	($953.20)	($43.81)
1/29/2014	Bank Deposit	$500.00	$456.19
1/29/2014	Satellite	($38.98)	$417.21
1/29/2014	Loan 2	($67.12)	$350.09
1/30/2014	VISA 2	($350.00)	$0.09

Chapter 9

Using a Spreadsheet to Track Progress

You should use a spreadsheet not only to keep track of your monthly recurring payments, but also to keep track of the progress you're making using the strategies in the chapters titled "Automatic Bill Payments" & "Using a Spreadsheet to Track Debts". You can use the spreadsheet to keep track of the balances of all of your loans, insurance premiums, credit cards, income, taxes (property and income) and past energy usage (gas, electric, phone and water). Keeping track of these expenses will help you see from month to month how you're doing in your struggle to spend less of your precious income. I keep all of this in one spreadsheet so all of this information is at my fingertips. I even keep track (within a month or two) of my debt payoff date. Doing this gives me a target date to aim for. Psychologically, this is a good thing, because without a goal to shoot for you will take much longer to pay your debts off and spend a great deal more in interest. The date may change, depending on events in your life, but at least if you stick to it you'll eventually get there. Below you will see a sample of this spreadsheet.

Diagram 4 - Sample Debt Calculator Spreadsheet – Total Debt

	Date	Mortgage	HELOC	Juniper Visa	TOTAL
	1/1/2014	($57,942.57)	($2,076.10)	($7,750.00)	($67,768.67)
	2/1/2014	($57,795.36)	($1,972.26)	($7,550.00)	($59,767.62)
	3/1/2014	($57,647.48)	($1,867.81)	($7,300.00)	($66,815.29)
	4/1/2014	($57,498.91)	($1,762.76)	($7,050.00)	($66,311.67)
	5/1/2014	($57,349.67)	($1,657.10)	($6,800.00)	($65,806.77)
2014	6/1/2014	($57,199.74)	($1,550.82)	($6,550.00)	($65,300.56)
	7/1/2014	($57,049.13)	($1,443.93)	($6,300.00)	($64,793.06)
	8/1/2014	($56,897.82)	($1,336.43)	($6,050.00)	($64,284.25)
	9/1/2014	($56,745.83)	($1,228.30)	($5,840.28)	($63,814.41)
	10/1/2014	($56,593.13)	($1,119.54)	($5,629.17)	($63,341.84)
	11/1/2014	($56,439.74)	($1,010.16)	($5,416.65)	($62,866.55)
	12/1/2014	($56,285.64)	($900.14)	($5,202.72)	($62,388.50)

Chapter 10

Useful Personal Finance Websites

Listed below are a number of useful and extremely educational websites – both for debt reduction and many other personal financial matters.

www.ConservativePersonalFinance.com – Site gives links to personal finance articles, personal finance advice and has products specifically tailored towards helping individuals get out of debt. This site is a companion to this book. There's a service included on the site where, for a minimum fee, we can use all your financial information (generic, of course, we don't want any information from you that can be stolen by hackers) to generate a report that's between 30 to 50 pages, depending on your situation, and shows where your money's being spent, how long it'll take to pay your debts off, how much extra you'll pay in interest, how much money you can save, etc. It also gives you alternative payoff dates depending on the percentage of reinvestment you choose to make. There are several charts and graphs to help you see exactly what's going on with your money. Finally, it gives you a payoff schedule based on YOUR debts and the information you give us.

www.Bankrate.com – For the best interest rates on credit cards, insurance, mortgages, and auto loans. Also has good advice about personal finance.

www.Smartmoney.com – Good personal finance advice. Includes advice about debt management and investments.

www.CBSMarketWatch.com – Investment, retirement, insurance and real estate advice. This site also has consumer advice on purchasing automobiles and other high ticket items.

www.foxnews.com – Good articles regarding personal finance. Extremely informative.

www.Freegrantsearch.com – Nice site, this site provides information on grants in all parts of the country that can be obtained for different purposes.

www.debtreliefcouncil.com – This site is similar to the one above, but provides alternative sources for grants.

www.Fool.com – Another good source for financial advice. This site deals specifically with investment but also has lots of excellent personal finance information.

www.gasbuddy.com – Through this site you can log onto more than 170 Web sites around the U.S. and in Canada that help consumers find cheap gas prices. Each site has a live forum for consumers to post local low and high gas prices they have found.

www.Newsmax.com – This website often has great articles on financial topics. Excellent site.

www.Kiplinger.com – Good personal finance advice. Includes advice about debt management and investments.

www.Money.CNN.com – Good retirement and personal finance advice. Very good resource.

www.Fortune.com – Mainly good for investment and retirement income advice.

www.ncpa.org – Good for general economic policy principles. Since all of our financial decisions are based on economic principles, it's good to have a basic understanding of how our economy works and the driving principles and forces behind it.

www.SBA.gov – Government website dedicated to helping small businesses get started. Provides information on start-up, and can help find/provide start-up capital.

Useful Personal Finance Software

Although the author cannot vouch for all of these personal finance programs, nor can he predict how any of you will like them, he has found some of these programs useful when trying to keep his finances in order. None of them, however, do ALL of the things that he wants. He has yet to find a program that covers all of the bases in a user-friendly fashion, one that's easy to use and also incorporates all of the functions he would like into one program. However, some of you may find that one or more of these are sufficient for your needs.

Mvelopes – www.mvelopes.com

Budgetmap – www.budgetmap.com

Quicken – www.quicken.com

Moneydance – www.moneydance.com

Budget Planner PRO – www.allpurposesoftware.com

MSMoney – www.microsoft.com/money

Credit Karma – www.creditkarma.com

Chapter 12

Other Sources of Income

Another way of increasing the speed with which you are able to pay off your debts and start saving is to increase your income. Sounds like a simple concept, but as we all know it's not so easy to do. There are a number of things you can do here; almost all of them will require hard work on your part, but then again, "Nothing worth having comes easy". A few ideas are listed below:

- Finish your education to secure a higher paying job.
- Get a second job.
- Ask your current employer for a raise.
- Try your hand at doing something on the Internet to increase your income. There are many things you can do on the Internet to increase your income (such as writing a guide like this), the trick is to find them.
- Invent something.
- Invest in real estate.

The drawback to all of these is that you really have to have money available to you, either your own or someone else's, to start. Often the government has grant and loan programs to help with this (the Small Business Administration is a great source of grants and loans for small businesses).

Local, county or federal low-income programs are also available, if necessary, and local charities are good sources of added income. We should earn our own way and not depend on other people. Sometimes, however, we have no choice and are forced to accept this. This is fine to get through tough times, but not so we can be lazy and never work again. We need to remember that the money is coming from someone else's hard work. Government handouts are not only bad for us personally, but they are bad for the economy and the country and are a HUGE part of the reason the federal and state budgets are so big. They're a big reason our taxes are so high. So, use them if you need them, but **ONLY** for as long as absolutely necessary to get back on good financial ground. Government grants mean financial dependence and loss of freedom, since grants normally come with strings attached. You really don't want to be dependent on anyone else for your well being. It's a great feeling being financially independent. Financial independence gives personal freedom.

Chapter 13

A Fit Body & Spirit for Healthy Finances

It's much cheaper to eat healthy food rather than spend your income on junk food. Carbohydrate-filled foods contribute to increased appetite. Eating foods like this don't keep hunger satisfied for long and they end up making you spend more money in a few hours to get more food. Eating a diet rich in protein, Omega-3 and 6 fatty acids, complex carbohydrates, nuts and unsaturated fats (fats like peanut oil, olive oil and canola oil) will help you to avoid those cravings and spend less money on food you just don't need. Evidence is emerging that this kind of diet is good for your heart, too.

Another component of a good personal finance plan is exercise. Proper exercise is as important as proper nutrition in avoiding wasted spending. When we get enough exercise, we feel better than when we don't, and that goes a long way toward spending less of our income on unnecessary food. We have within us all the equipment we need to get plenty of exercise. We don't need expensive workout equipment or gym memberships to accomplish this. Walking is a very good exercise and it's easy to do. Jogging, if done carefully, can also be very good for you physically and psychologically. Of course, you should not try anything strenuous until you have been seen by a physician and obtained his approval.

Last, but not least, a word about God. Since He is the one who gave us all we have and will ever have, it is only appropriate that we look to Him for guidance and thank Him for what He has given us. A few minutes of prayer, attending church regularly and making sure live a good life will help us to see more clearly what it is that God wants for us. Following His commandments will naturally lead you to better personal finance, as many of the things He has told us to do are things like not over eating and not wasting money frivolously. These things cost money, and lots of it. So let's all do what God has commanded and we'll all be better for it, financially and spiritually. Indeed, since the Commandments are really simply very wise rules of human social conduct, widespread violation of them undermines the social stability of both family and society, thereby costing individuals, families, and society as a whole many billions of dollars attempting often ill-conceived social remedies that fail to work and only add greatly to the national debt and taxpayer burdens.

Chapter 14

Saving Money and Charitable Donations

Once you have used all of these techniques to eliminate your debt, you need to start saving money. Make your money work for you now. Invest it, save it, hide it under your mattress. Whatever you do, don't let yourself go back into debt and don't waste money. Save every dollar possible. You will find that the wealthiest people often are the ones who pinch every penny.

While you need to save, save, save, you also ought to give to charity. Give to your church and also to charities you believe in, check them out and make sure they're doing what they say they're doing, then give them a percentage of your income. God wants us to be charitable; this is a good way to do that. There are many who are less fortunate than we are.

A percentage of all profits from sales on this book and from any other products associated with Conservative Personal Finance gets donated to charities that we believe are deserving and provide a needed and positive contribution to society.

Conclusion

We all seem to, at one time or another, have trouble with our finances. This happens because we are not careful enough about where we spend our money. It happens because we're not taught at a young age how to take care of our finances. This needs to be taught by our parents and schools. Personal Finance courses ought to be taught in every high school in the nation.

It's hard to be diligent about finances, but that is exactly what we need to be these days. We need to be very frugal and conservative so we don't find ourselves in a position that we can't get out of easily. We live on the edge, spending our money so fast that by the next paycheck we have nothing left. That's not the way to live. The stress from debt can be enormous and can have lasting negative effects on your health and personal relationships.

The following list gives the main points covered in this guide:

1. Pray to God for guidance

2. Reduce your spending (Chapter 4)

3. Make a spending plan (Chapter 5)

4. Use the roll-down method to pay off debt (Chapter 6)

5. Have a set amount (debt payments plus an extra amount) deducted from your pay and direct deposited into an account designated for paying down debts and paying bills (Chapter 7)

6. Track your debts and progress with a spreadsheet (Chapters 8 & 9)

7. Learn as much as you can about personal finance from websites and libraries

8. Find other sources of income to supplement what you already make (Chapter 10)

9. Keep checking on things and don't get behind or lazy about your finances

10. Get plenty of exercise and eat healthy

11. Save and invest the monthly payments to protect your future

12. Give to charities and church

Using the strategies outlined in this guide, before you know it you'll be well on your way to saving and making money from your income, rather than giving it to creditors. You'll have the freedom to go on the vacation you've always wanted, send your kids to college or buy a new house, all without using high interest credit to do it. Good Luck!!

ABOUT THE AUTHOR

Gregory Bonnette has been dealing with, and writing about, debt issues for over 15 years. He's experienced in using unique debt elimination strategies to help challenged clients get out of debt fast. Not only is he the author of debt elimination guides, but he's also developed a unique product designed to create an individual debt elimination plan for each unique client.

www.ingramcontent.com/pod-product-compliance
Lightning Source LLC
Chambersburg PA
CBHW041613180526
45159CB00002BC/842